THE UNOFFICIAL GUIDE TO
GOAL SETTING IN MINECRAFT®

JILL KEPPELER

Published in 2026 by The Rosen Publishing Group, Inc.
2544 Clinton Street, Buffalo, NY 14224

Copyright © 2026 by The Rosen Publishing Group, Inc.

All rights reserved. No part of this book may be reproduced in any form without permission in writing from the publisher, except by a reviewer.

First Edition

Editor: Greg Roza
Book Design: Rachel Rising
Illustrator: Matías Lapegüe

Photo Credits: Cover, p. 1 Soloma/Shutterstock.com; Cover, pp. 1, 5, 7, 8, 11, 12, 14, 16, 18, 20, 22–24 Oksana Kalashnykova/Shutterstock.com; Cover, pp. 1, 3, 6–8, 10–12, 14, 16, 18, 20, 22–24 SkillUp/Shutterstock.com; Cover, pp. 1, 5, 7, 8, 11, 12, 14, 16, 18, 20 gersamina donnichi/Shutterstock.com; p. 5 Prostock-studio/Shutterstock.com.

Library of Congress Cataloging-in-Publication Data

Names: Keppeler, Jill author
Title: The unofficial guide to goal setting in Minecraft / Jill Keppeler.
Description: Buffalo : PowerKids Press, 2026. | Series: The unofficial guide to Minecraft social skills | Includes index.
Identifiers: LCCN 2025005211 (print) | LCCN 2025005212 (ebook) | ISBN 9781499452884 library binding | ISBN 9781499452877 paperback | ISBN 9781499452891 ebook
Subjects: LCSH: Minecraft (Game)–Juvenile literature | Goal (Psychology)–Juvenile literature
Classification: LCC GV1469.35.M535 K4582 2026 (print) | LCC GV1469.35.M535 (ebook) | DDC 794.8/5–dc23/eng/20250416
LC record available at https://lccn.loc.gov/2025005211
LC ebook record available at https://lccn.loc.gov/2025005212

Manufactured in the United States of America

Minecraft is a trademark of Mojang (a game development studio owned by Microsoft Technology Corporation), and its use in this book does not imply a recommendation or endorsement of this title by Mojang or Microsoft.

Some of the images in this book illustrate individuals who are models. The depictions do not imply actual situations or events.

CPSIA Compliance Information: Batch #CSPK26. For Further Information contact Rosen Publishing at 1-800-237-9932.

CONTENTS

SLAY THAT DRAGON! 4
WHAT DO YOU WANT? 6
SMALLER STEPS 8
WHAT'S IN THE WAY? 10
TAKING A PAUSE 12
STAY FOCUSED 14
TEAM GOALS 16
YOU CAN DO IT! 20
GLOSSARY 22
FOR MORE INFORMATION 23
INDEX 24

SLAY THAT DRAGON!

With a lot of games, the goal is simple. Get the most points. Save the princess. Build a successful city. Defeat the dark lord. *Minecraft* is different. There's no end point! Your goals depend on you.

Maybe you want to play in creative **mode** and build a copy of your favorite movie spaceship. Or maybe you want to build up your **resources** and **slay** the ender dragon, the closest thing the game has to a big boss. But to do these things, you need to know what you want and work for it. It's important to set goals to get things done.

MINECRAFT MANIA

The ender dragon is a giant flying creature in the End, a unique, or one-of-a-kind, *Minecraft* **dimension**. It takes a lot of work and resources even to get there!

One cool point about *Minecraft* is that it can be many different things. It all depends on what you want to do.

WHAT DO YOU WANT?

The first step in setting goals, of course, is to know what you want. This seems easy, right? But take your time and think about it. When you start a new *Minecraft* world, what are you hoping to do? Build something? Fight enemies? Play with friends? Explore and find a particular **biome**? It may be a combination of these things!

Start with setting your biggest goal. Say you want to play by yourself, find a jungle biome, build a treehouse base, and then find the End and defeat the ender dragon. Now you have a good start!

MINECRAFT MANIA

 There are three kinds of jungle biomes in *Minecraft*: regular jungle, **sparse** jungle, and bamboo jungle.

Minecraft jungle trees are the tallest trees in the game. They can be up to 31 blocks tall! The biggest trees won't be in the sparse jungle biome, though.

SMALLER STEPS

Once you've set your big goal, you need to break it down into smaller pieces. You can't go right to beating the ender dragon when you just dropped into a new *Minecraft* world! Think about the steps it will take to get there and then set about doing them one at a time.

Your first step in the stated goal would be to find a jungle biome, unless you **spawned** in one. Of course, this is after the usual early *Minecraft* goals like getting basic tools, weapons, and food and surviving your first nights.

MINECRAFT MANIA

Most goals will have smaller goals in them. One of the first things to do in a *Minecraft* survival world is to find trees, get some wood, and make basic tools, like a pickaxe!

WHAT'S IN THE WAY?

Next, you need to identify, or name, the **obstacles** in the way in toward meeting your goals. For example, if you're looking for a jungle biome, you'll want to be sure you're not going in circles. There are a few good ways to do this. You can make a map or a compass. Maybe you'll want both!

You might have to explore a long way to find a jungle biome. That can be an obstacle too. You might get **discouraged**. This is normal. What's important is how you deal with it. It might be worth pausing to think about things.

MINECRAFT MANIA

 You can make a regular map in *Minecraft* with nine pieces of paper. With a compass and eight pieces of paper, you can make a map that always shows your location when you're in that area.

A *Minecraft* compass will point back to your spawn point. You can use it to find your way back there—or if you're exploring, to be sure you're always moving away.

TAKING A PAUSE

Let's say you've explored your world for days—real days, not *Minecraft* ones! You're discouraged you haven't found a jungle biome. Maybe you've found a cool different place to build, like near a village or above a resource-filled mineshaft.

It's OK to stop and think about your goals, whether they're in the real world or in *Minecraft*. Is building a jungle base still what you want? It's OK to decide that staying in the village would better help you reach your big goal. But if you decide you really do want that jungle base, you can then work on what you want to do next.

MINECRAFT MANIA

Carrying all your resources with you in *Minecraft* for a long time can be tough. If you have a donkey, llama, or mule with you, though, they can help carry things.

Villages can have some helpful resources. There are villagers to trade with, premade buildings, and sometimes, chests with loot.

STAY FOCUSED

So, you've searched and searched, keeping track of your location with maps and a compass, and you finally found your jungle biome! You picked out a tall jungle tree and carefully built yourself the perfect treehouse. It feels good to reach a goal, doesn't it? It's OK to be proud!

Don't let it **distract** you from your big goal, though. To get to the End and beat the ender dragon, you'll need lots of resources and the best weapons. You'll also have more searching to do to find a stronghold and an End **portal**. Are you ready?

MINECRAFT MANIA

Strongholds are underground structures, or buildings. They're the only place End portals can be found, but they may also have libraries full of bookshelves and other rooms.

Strongholds can be very much like a maze. It's important to keep track of where you've explored while in one.

TEAM GOALS

In some cases, you can also play *Minecraft* online or in person with your friends. This can be fun and very helpful for reaching goals, but it also means there are further things to think about when setting them. What if not everyone has the same goals? Can you reach an agreement about setting your team's goals while still having each person's goals?

Sometimes a big team goal just won't work out, and that's OK. If a few people want to battle the ender dragon and a few people just want to build cool things and explore, it's better to know before you all start playing together.

MINECRAFT MANIA

One way teams can work together to get to the End and beat the ender dragon is to find ender pearls. Players can use these (with blaze powder) to make eyes of ender, which can lead you to strongholds.

Ender portals also need eyes of ender to activate, or start, them. You might need one to 12 eyes of ender. It's very, very rare not to need any.

Once you're in the End, your goal is at hand. You and your friends can use teamwork to beat the ender dragon. Everyone will need a role, or part. Some people might use bows (or a crossbow) and arrows to break the end crystals the dragon uses to heal and attack the dragon when it's in the air. Some people can focus on using powerful swords to attack the dragon when it lands. Still others might hold healing **potions** to help everyone else.

It might take more than one try, but when you beat the dragon, it's time to celebrate!

MINECRAFT MANIA

You may want to go to the outer islands in the End to get some unique loot. You may want to go back to your base and build it up even more. Now is the time to make new goals!

The ender dragon has 200 health points! A regular player with no armor or potions has only 20.

YOU CAN DO IT!

This should give you a good idea about how to set up goals, think about them, and meet them. You might have goals that are only your own, or you might have team goals that you and friends work on together. It's likely you'll have both.

In *Minecraft* or in real life, it's important to think about your goals. For example, you might want to set a goal to get better grades in a class. The same things apply: think about what you want, identify the smaller steps, and know your obstacles. If you try, you can do almost anything!

Another possible goal in *Minecraft* is to beat the wither. This enemy is even tougher to beat than the ender dragon! It has 300 to 600 health points.

There are so many goals you can set in *Minecraft*. You can reach the lowest point in the underground or climb the highest peak you can find!

GLOSSARY

biome: A natural community of plants and animals, such as a forest or desert.

dimension: A level of existence.

discouraged: Feeling without courage or confidence.

distract: To draw away attention.

mode: A version, or form of something that is different from others.

obstacle: Something that stops forward movement or progress.

portal: A door or entrance.

potion: A drink meant to have a magical effect on someone.

resource: Something that can be used.

slay: To kill.

sparse: Having few or scattered things.

spawn: To first appear.

FOR MORE INFORMATION

BOOKS

Battista, Brianna. *Planning for Success: Goal Setting*. PowerKids Press: Buffalo, NY: 2019.

Mojang AB. *Minecraft: Guide to Exploration*. Random House Worlds: 2023.

Tauszik, Karleen. *Every Kid's Guide to Goals*. Karleen Tauszik, 2017.

WEBSITES

The End
minecraft.wiki/w/The_End
Learn more about the Minecraft dimension called The End and how to get there on the Minecraft Wiki.

What Can You Mine with Minecraft?
wonderopolis.org/wonder/What-Can-You-Mine-with-Minecraft
Learn more about Minecraft (and goals in the game) with Wonderopolis.

Publisher's note to educators and parents: Our editors have carefully reviewed these websites to ensure that they are suitable for students. Many websites change frequently, however, and we cannot guarantee that a site's future contents will continue to meet our high standards of quality and educational value. Be advised that students should be closely supervised whenever they access the internet.

INDEX

B
biomes, 6, 7, 8, 10, 12, 14

E
End, the, 5, 6, 14, 16, 18

F
friends, 6, 16, 18, 20

M
map and compass, 10, 11, 14

O
obstacle, 10, 11, 20

P
pause, 10, 12
portal, 14, 17
potion, 18, 19

R
resources, 4, 5, 12, 13, 14

T
team, 16, 18, 20

V
village, 12, 13